MATH WORDS AND SYMBOLS

Lynn Peppas

Crabtree Publishing Company

www.crabtreebooks.com

Author: Lynn Peppas
Coordinating editor: Chester Fisher
Series editor: Penny Dowdy
Editor: Reagan Miller
Proofreader: Ellen Rodger
Editorial director: Kathy Middleton
Production coordinator: Margaret Amy Salter
Prepress technician: Margaret Amy Salter
Cover design: Samara Parent
Logo design: Samantha Crabtree
Project manager: Kumar Kunal (Q2AMEDIA)
Art direction: Dibakar Acharjee (Q2AMEDIA)
Design: Harleen Mehta (Q2AMEDIA)
Photo research: Anju Pathak (Q2AMEDIA)

Photographs:
123RF: Ivan Gulei: p. 8 (left); Juana Van Burg: p. 10; Milos Luzanin:
    p. 19; Plistserv: p. 14 (left); Andrjuss Soldatovs: p. 16 (left);
    Ints Vikmanis: p. 16 (right)
Dreamstime: Bellat: p. 21; Wandakrack: p. 14 (right)
Q2AMedia Art Bank: p9, 13, 15, 17
Rex Features: Alex Segre: p. 7
Shutterstock: Baevskiy Dmitry: p. 9, 13, 15; Barbro Bergfeldt: p. 11 (top);
    Diamond Images: p. 1; Ebtikar: p. 19; Gelpi: front cover; Joanne Harris and
    Daniel Bubnich: p. 1; Georgios Kollidas: folio image; Kuzma: p. 12 (right),
    23 (right); Lana Langlois: p. 12 (left), 23 (left); Jean Morrison: p. 5;
    Anita Patterson Peppers: p. 1; Stephen Aaron Rees: p. 5; Tina Rencelj:
    p. 8 (right); Elena Schweitzer: p. 20 (left); Semjonow Juri : p. 20; Carolina K.
    Smith, M.D: p. 1; Danny Smythe: p. 11 (top); Brian Weed: p. 17

Library and Archives Canada Cataloguing in Publication

Peppas, Lynn
     Math words and symbols / Lynn Peppas.

(My path to math)
Includes index.
ISBN 978-0-7787-4347-7 (bound).--ISBN 978-0-7787-4365-1 (pbk.)

     1. Mathematical notation--Juvenile literature. I. Title.
II. Series: My path to math

QA41.P46 2009   j510   C2009-903580-4

Library of Congress Cataloging-in-Publication Data

Peppas, Lynn.
  Math words and symbols / Lynn Peppas.
     p. cm. -- (My path to math)
  Includes index.
  ISBN 978-0-7787-4347-7 (reinforced lib. bdg. : alk. paper)
-- ISBN 978-0-7787-4365-1 (pbk. : alk. paper)
  1. Mathematical notation--Juvenile literature. I. Title. II. Series.

  QA41.P447 2010
  510--dc22

                                                  2009022856

Crabtree Publishing Company
www.crabtreebooks.com   1-800-387-7650

Published in Canada
Crabtree Publishing
616 Welland Ave.
St. Catharines, ON
L2M 5V6

Published in the United States
Crabtree Publishing
PMB16A
350 Fifth Ave., Suite 3308
New York, NY 10118

Published in the United Kingdom
Crabtree Publishing
Lorna House, Suite 3.03, Lorna Road
Hove, East Sussex, UK
BN3 3EL

Published in Australia
Crabtree Publishing
386 Mt. Alexander Rd.
Ascot Vale (Melbourne)
VIC 3032

Contents

Symbols and Words

People talk about math every day. We talk about math at school. We use math in our homes and at work. Math words let us talk about something we can count or measure.

We write about math, too. A math **symbol** is a sign. It stands for something counted or measured. Math symbols help us write less when we write about math.

Fact Box

Numbers are math symbols that tell us an **amount**.

1 for $ 1

4 for

3 for $ 5

3 for $ 2

2 for $ 1

Numbers and symbols tell us how much the fruit costs.

Number Sentences

A sentence has words. The words tell us stories or ideas. You are reading a sentence right now!

Number sentences work the same way. But they do not use words. Number sentences use math symbols. A number sentence tells us about things we can count. This is a number sentence:

1 + 1 = 2

Math symbols show how we **compare** groups. The symbols tell us if two amounts are the same or different.

Fact Box

Number sentences tell us about a math **problem**. Writing the problem helps us understand it.

Numbers tell us about things we can count.

Equal

Aaron helps his grandmother shop.
His grandmother needs to buy oranges.
Aaron picks out three oranges. His
grandmother picks out three oranges too.

They compare their groups of oranges.
Aaron's group has the same amount as his
grandmother's group. The groups are **equal**.
An equal sign shows the groups are the same.

$$3 = 3$$

three oranges equals three oranges

Activity Box

Draw two groups of oranges. The groups should
be equal. Put an equal sign between the groups.

Equal groups have the same number in them.

Not Equal

Aaron's grandmother wants to buy pears. Aaron picks two pears from the pile. His grandmother picks five pears.

They compare their groups of pears. Aaron and his grandmother have different amounts. The amounts are not the same. So they are **not equal**. A not equal sign shows the groups are not the same.

 $2 \neq 5$

two pears do not equal five pears

Activity Box

Draw two groups of pears that are not equal. Put a not equal sign between the two groups.

Groups that are not equal do not have the same number in them. Are these two groups of pears equal, or not equal?

Greater Than

Aaron picks out six bananas. His grandmother takes four bananas. She asks him, "Which group has more?" To find out, Aaron compares the two groups.

Aaron counts his group. Then he counts his grandmother's group. Aaron's group has more bananas. So Aaron's group is **greater than** his grandmother's group. A greater than sign shows that one group has more than another.

$$6 > 4$$

six bananas are greater than four bananas

Fact Box

Think of the greater-than symbol as a crocodile's mouth. The crocodile opens its mouth toward the bigger number to eat it.

We must compare two groups to see if one is greater than the other.

Less Than

Aaron gets two green apples. His grandmother gets four red apples. Which group has **less than** the other?

Aaron and his grandmother count the apples. Then they compare the two groups. Two is less than four. Aaron's group is less than his grandmother's. A less than sign shows that one group has fewer than another.

2 < 4

two is less than four

Fact Box

Always put the point of the less than sign next to the smaller number.

We must compare two groups to see if one is less than the other.

Adding

Aaron picks out three carrots. His grandmother picks out four carrots. How many in all?

Aaron can add the groups. He counts the carrots in both groups of carrots. There are seven carrots in all.

Aaron can use a **plus sign** to write his math problem. A plus sign is a math symbol. It looks like this: +. It shows that groups are being added together.

$$3 + 4 = 7$$

*three plus four
equals seven*

Activity Box

When you add, the answer is called the **sum**.

How many carrots does Aaron have altogether?

Subtracting

Aaron's grandmother needs six carrots. But Aaron brings her seven carrots. Aaron has too many carrots. He must put some carrots back.

Aaron must subtract the carrots he does not need. He starts with the group they have. He takes away the extra carrot. Aaron knows he needs to use a minus sign to write this math problem. A **minus sign** is a math symbol. It looks like this: −. It shows that Aaron subtracted.

Fact Box

When you subtract, the answer is called the **difference**.

seven minus one equals six

When we take one carrot away, what is the difference?

Dollars and Cents

Dollars and **cents** are math words. They help us talk about money.

A dollar is 100 pennies. We use a dollar sign when something costs 100 pennies or more. It looks like this: $.

We use the cents sign when something costs less than one dollar. The cents sign looks like this: ¢.

Activity Box

A watermelon costs three dollars. What symbol would you use? A pear costs 75 cents. What symbol would you use?

Can you find dollar and cent symbols in the picture?

Glossary

amount   A number or value

cents   ¢; An amount of money that is less than one dollar

compare   To see what is the same or different

difference   The answer when numbers are subtracted

dollar $; An amount of money equal to 100 pennies

equal   =; Two or more groups with the same amount

greater than   >; More than another amount

less than   <; Fewer than another amount

minus sign –; A symbol that tells you to subtract

not equal ≠; Two or more groups that have different amounts

plus sign +; A symbol that tells you to add

problem A question that needs an answer

sum The answer when numbers are added

symbol A sign that stands for something

6 > 4

Index

Printed in the U.S.A. — BG